BOOKS ON DEMAND

AN EXHIBITION *OF* TWELVE ILLUSTRATED BOOKS
PRODUCED USING PRINT-ON-DEMAND SERVICES

—

by ZOË SADOKIERSKI

—

CONTENTS

PROLOGUE

PART 1 —
BOOKS DESIGNED
for PRINT-ON-DEMAND
PRODUCTION

—

Analogue Bodies Vol. 1:
Feet and Teeth.
Collection of 3 illustrated books
Collaboration with Tom Lee
2014

—

Words from the First Walk
Exhibition catalogue and book
Collaboration with Tom Lee
and Jacquie Lorber-Kasunic
2013

—

Mariposa
Exhibition catalogue
Collaboration with George Plionis
2014

—

Viva La Novella series
Four illustrated book covers
Commissioned by Seizure (publisher)
2014

—

PART 2 —
WORK REFORMATTED
for PRINT-ON-DEMAND
PRODUCTION

—

A Poetics of the Naughty
Illustrated book
Collaboration with Tom Lee
2012 / 2014

—

Birds with Smutty Names
Illustrated book
2012 / 2014

—

Writers' Typewriters
Illustrated book
2011 / 2014

—

PROLOGUE

—

Books On Demand is an exhibition of 12 limited-edition illustrated books, produced using print-on-demand services. Also exhibited are the prototypes and graphic experiments created as part of my design process.

Print-on-demand services allow anyone with a computer and credit card to quickly and cheaply self-publish a book. The process is simple: the publisher (in this instance, me) uploads digital files (PDFs of the internal pages and cover) to an online platform (the print-on-demand service provider). Then when someone orders a book, it is printed, bound and delivered anywhere in the world within in a few days.

Print-on-demand has existed for a number of years, primarily as a service for printing 'photobooks' (family and wedding photo albums) and cheaply produced paperback books for self-published authors. More recently companies such as Blurb and Lulu have introduced high quality colour printing on specialty paper-stocks and additional finishing/binding options, transforming print-on-demand from 'quick and cheap' to a viable publishing model for well-produced books.

The 12 books in this exhibition were produced using a variety of different print-on-demand formats and service providers, to test the range of publishing options available. Some of the books were designed specifically for print-on-demand production – *Analogue Bodies* (2014), *Words from the First Walk* (2013), *Mariposa* (2014), the Viva La Novella series (published by Seizure, 2014) – and others were originally artworks or artist's books that I have reformatted as print-on-demand books – *Birds with Smutty Names* (2012/2014); *A Poetics of the Naughty* (2012/2014), and; *Writer's Typewriters* (2011/2014). The books are a mix of commercial projects, exhibition catalogues and research experiments.

This catalogue documents the design and production process behind each book, and makes clear what is gained – and what is lost – using this publishing technology.

LESS WASTE, MORE PROFIT

Traditional off-set book printers rarely print fewer than 1000 books in a print-run. The large quantities are cost driven:

setting up printing presses and binding machines takes time (human labour) and resources (electricity, paper, inks, for some presses also water). The cost of these overheads is distributed across the quantity of books printed, so the more books printed, the cheaper the unit-price per book.

This production model carries financial problems for niche publishers and authors who self-publish. Printing large quantities of stock before a market has been established for the book means storing cartons of books that may never be sold. The books need to be stored somewhere, and warehousing and distribution (getting the books to shops or individual customers) incur extra fees. If the publisher can't sell the stock they struggle to break even, let alone make a profit.

Then there's the waste issue; what to do with leftover stock? Large publishers periodically send trucks to bookstores to collect unsold stock and ferry it back to warehouses, usually in remote locations; petrol, emissions, and labour costs ensue. There, the unsold books are pulped (some of which is recycled as cardboard) a process that requires large quantities of chemicals, electricity and water. Waste begets more waste. Small publishers don't have these facilities, which means collecting unsold books in person, incurring further time and resource costs and making 'bricks-and-mortar' shops less likely to stock small publishers' books because it requires more admin work on everyone's part. And the problem of what to do with excess stock remains.

Here lies the value of print-on-demand. Many print-on-demand providers will print as few as a single copy of a book and deliver it anywhere in the world. In some cases, this is achievable using machines that digitally print and bind an individual book quickly and efficiently, consuming less time and resources than traditional printers. The internal pages of 300-page book can be printed in less than a minute. In other cases, the printer specifies standard book sizes (for example trade paperback, or A5) and prints a collection of books set up in the same standard size at once – although only one copy of your book is printed, numerous other books the same size are produced at the same time, reducing overheads. Both models are possible because of advancements in digital printing technology.

OPENING THE MARKET *for* NICHE PUBLISHERS

The rise of print-on-demand has lead to a boom in independent publishing internationally. The quick, inexpensive, and less wasteful production model offered by print-on-demand allows publishers with smaller or less established audiences to break into the market.

In Australia, the Small Press Network (SPN), a not-for-profit incorporation with a mission to "promote independent publishing and support the principle of diversity within the publishing industry as a vital component of Australian literary culture" was formed in 2006. http://spunc.com.au

The Small Press Network has more than 120 publisher members and is hosting its second 'Ind Pub' conference in Sydney, November 13–14 2014, where I will speak about the research behind the **Books On Demand** project.

Broadly, my research is concerned with the evolution of the book in a digital age, from a design perspective. In particular, considering how the role of the designer could change in emerging publishing models:

— What happens when designers are consulted in earlier (project development) stages of the publishing process?

— How could a designer's particular understanding of word-image interplay and materiality alter the way books are conceived, designed and produced?

— What opportunities does digital production technology afford the designer in the publishing process?

Books On Demand reports on a series of projects – the 12 books and the collection of prototypes that led to their production – in which I address these questions through commercial and creative design practice. I consider this work the first iteration of an ongoing investigation, which I anticipate will continue for years to come.

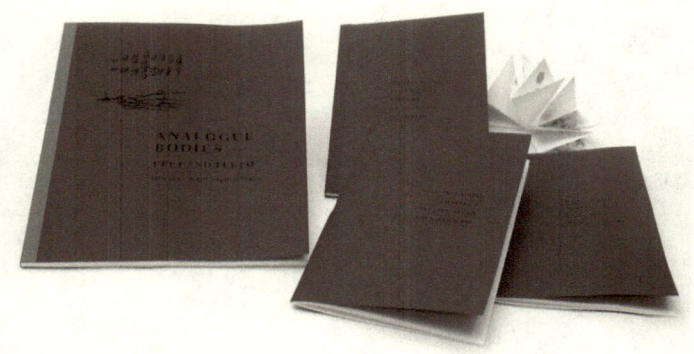

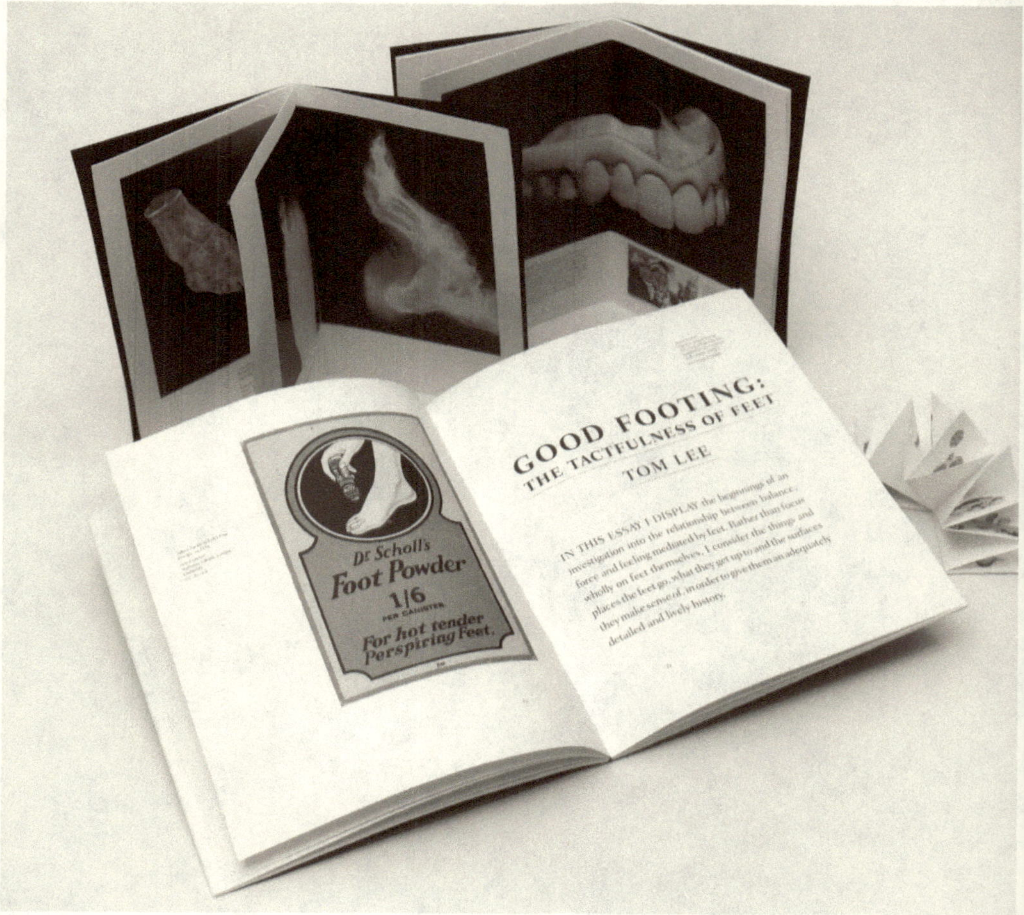

ANALOGUE BODIES

VOL. 1: FEET AND TEETH

Essays by Tom Lee.

Visual essays and artist's books
by Zoë Sadokierski.

PROJECT DESCRIPTION

Analogue Bodies: Vol. 1 is a collection of essays by Tom Lee, materialised as a set of illustrated books by Zoë Sadokierski; a true collaboration between a writer and a designer. It looks at different parts of, and events within, the human body and historical ways of depicting and making sense of them. It aims to humour and, on its day, to educate.

The first iteration of the project was presented at the Emerging Writers' Festival in Melbourne, 27 May – 6 June 2014. The work was the centrepiece of the 'Reading Room' at The Wheeler Centre for the duration of the festival, with a launch in which Tom and Zoë discussed their collaboration. At this stage, there were six books: the main book with Tom's essays on feet and teeth, and; five 'anti-chapters' – handmade books Zoë produced in response to Tom's essays, which belong to the main book like a shadow belongs to a body:

The second iteration was produced as a print-on-demand edition of the main book and three of the anti-chapters.

During the collaboration, Tom's essay on feet was published in *Higher Arc*, issue 4, featuring illustrations by Zoë. http://higherarc.com/issue-4/

Following the Festival, *Cordite Poetry Review* published an interview with Tom and Zoë about the collaboration featuring images of the work: 'Analogue Bodies: A conversation with Tom Lee and Zoë Sadokierski', 10 July 2014. 2pp. http://cordite.org.au/guncotton/analogue-bodies/

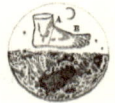

IN BETWEEN THE SOLE AND THE GROUND
—

Our vision, and by extension our *visions*, might be preoccupied with the horizon in the distance, the adventures we are yet to have beyond the limit between landscape and sky. However, there is another meeting point that is of more immediate importance: *what's beneath our feet*. There is an entire world of feelings, forces and forms that come between our feet and the ground.

Our hands and fingers are to a large extent free from the pervasive pressure of gravity to which our feet and bottoms are regularly subject. The sense of touch associated with our hands is closely acquainted with delicacy and lightness, with tactfulness, which means to touch lightly and to generally be discreet. By contrast, we feel the weightiness of our bodies through our feet, and through movement we transfer this weightiness as force. Feet are commonly viewed as implements that damage or spread dirt. 'Tread lightly', we are told. 'Don't tread on us', we threaten. However, the forcefulness of the foot does not limit the delights and disgusts it can provoke. Feet are also closely implicated with extreme sensitivity, and, inevitably, with pleasure and pain.

Although we primarily walk *on* surfaces and feel downward in this sense, our feet also gives us a sense of buoyancy, of bounce, roll, and spring. The body works *with* gravity and weight in grinding, crunching, stomping and stamping; resists it through leaping, springing and climbing; and is subject to it as we slip, stumble, sink and fall.

Type 'crushing under foot' into the search tab in Youtube and witness the results. There are extensive series of foot crushing videos that feature all manner of objects subject to tantilising degradation at the hands of the feet: the slow pummeling of a plump iceberg lettuce into a motely of wet flakes, the sticky pulverisation of seedy figs on the pavement, the crackle of crackers into powdery fragments, the liquid squish of cherry tomatos, watermelon, grapes and strawberries, as wells as mashed sausages, cake, dung, Twinkies, hardboiled eggs, pizza

PROJECT AIMS

Tom's aims, from the introduction to the main book:

> *I was a writer, more specifically,*
> **someone writing essays with a commit-**
> **ment to the idea that poetic thinking is**
> **essential in providing things with**
> **adequate and lively histories. ...**
> *This series is an examination of the human body piece*
> *by piece, with each part spun through sequences of*
> *sentences and paragraphs.*

Broadly, my aim was to visualise/materialise Tom's essays to get them into the hands of more readers, as stated in the introduction:

> *Tom's essays connect things in unexpected ways. I*
> *find myself surprised, delighted, entertained,*
> *informed and inspired – all the reasons I read. When*
> *there is so much content flying around, how can we*
> *determine what's worth making time to stop and read*
> *fully, rather than skimming or filing away for some*
> *vaguely anticipated later, less busy moment?*

By materialising Tom's essays – giving them a physical form and extending them with images and extra texts – I hope to attract more readers to these excellent pieces of writing. This is the best gift a designer can offer a writer whose work she admires.

In a research context, my more specific aims were to:

1. Document our collaborative process, by saving all digital correspondence and process work in order to reflect back on it later. Tom and I have successfully collaborated for several years – *why does this collaboration work, and how can we grow it from here?*;

2. Test print-on-demand as a publishing model for creative work. Our earlier collaborations found audience – *how could I design this work to be easily reproducible, for people to buy?*

3. Use Creative Commons licensed material to illustrate the books – *how could archival images allow me to illustrate texts in new ways?* This is an ongoing research strand that feeds into much of my recent design practice, in both commercial and experimental projects.

DESIGN STRATEGY

To illustrate Tom's essays I sourced images from the Wellcome Collection, a medical science museum in London, supplemented by additional images from the online archive Vintage Printable. The aim was to visually communicate the research and rigour underpinning Tom's writing, by using photographs and medical illustrations that carry a sense of scientific authority. My own illustration style is not sufficiently technical to pull this off, which is why I chose to use archival images. However, the images I have chosen are all in some way odd or surprising, reflecting the tone and playfulness of Tom's writing style.

I am able to use these images because they have been released under Creative Commons licenses. These new licenses allow designers to use archival images, even for commercial purposes, if the copyright has lapsed or the copyright holder permits their reuse. Current digital scanning and reproduction technologies allow cultural institutions such as the Wellcome Collection to release archival images (digital reproductions of photographs, paintings and other images from their collection) using Creative Commons licenses, opening their collections to wider audiences. Creative Commons licenses have the potential to change the

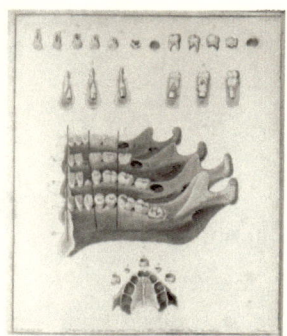

20.

way designers work in publishing, by affording access to rich archives of previously inaccessible material for free. See: www.creativecommons.org.au

While sourcing these images – I searched for 'feet', 'teeth' and variations on these words such as 'mouth', 'dental', 'oral hygiene' – I uncovered an enormous quantity of fascinating visual material. The images I used alongside Tom's essays all relate to an idea or object described in his text. The images are placed in close proximity to the related text, to point the reader to the connection. These are occasionally obvious – a medical engraving titled 'Teeth of a child at various ages' next to the passage "Few people wouldn't recall some residual sensation of the fascinating and perturbing childhood experience of a wobbly tooth" – and other times more obscure – alongside a description of the humanoid aliens from James Cameron's film Avatar, I place a drawing titled 'Three unusual looking men' from the 17th Century that look uncannily like Cameron's aliens. It doesn't directly illustrate Tom's writing, but extends it through new visual information.

I created other illustrations by collaging several images together, to reinforce a point. For example, Tom is troubled to discover that teeth are not "hard little rocks" but hollow and composed of "a dense tubular stuff known as 'dentine'. Like

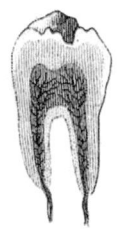

oranges and lemons, teeth contain pulp." Juxtaposed drawings of the interior of a tooth and a lemon reinforce Tom's description. Tom continues his uncomfortable analysis: "Indeed, it is more reassuring to think of a tooth as a densely resistant pebble than as a potentially homely shell. This idea now calls to mind the experience of abject horror that I felt when discovering a small, translucent crab nested in a muscle shell that I expected to house only muscle." Alongside this passage I place an illustration of the same tooth, now juxtaposed with the interior of a crab. Mirrored across the double page spread, these two illustrations link Tom's writing and aim to visually extend the 'abject horror' he describes.

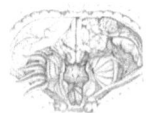

21.

———

Searching the archives, some images seemed too remarkable to omit, despite being only tangentially connected to Tom's essays. While I snuck in a couple of images (such as the Avatar-alien), I decided the majority were more 'anti-chapter' material because they required the meta-data and information from the catalogue notes (from the Wellcome archive) to be fully appreciated, and I was cautious of distracting the reader from Tom's essays by adding substantial amounts of additional text.

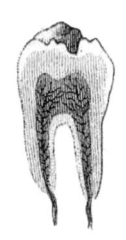

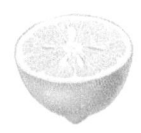

Collaged by Zoë Sadokierski from Köhler's Medizinal Pflanzen, 1887 (lemon); Dr H.G. Bronn's Crab Circulatory System, 1866 (crab) and tooth from coloured engraving by A. Tardieu.

IMAGE CREDITS:
Lemon and crab: www. vintageprintable.com and tooth: Wellcome Library, London

Instead, I created two visual essays that sit alongside the main book, titled 'Small Feet' – a sequence of images related to Chinese foot-binding, and 'Pulling Teeth' – a collection of images related to dental hygiene, including some bizarre

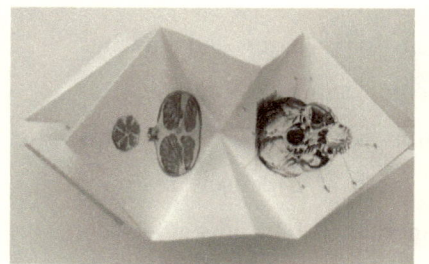 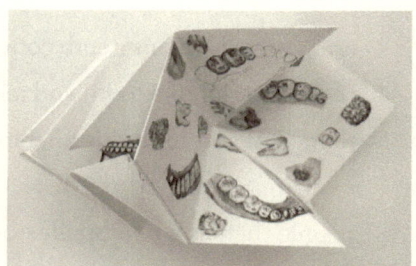

Flower-fold
teeth book

superstitious practices. The visual essays belong to the Analogue Bodies project without detracting from Tom's essays – they are smaller format books than the 'main book' to show they are less important.

In the early stages of playing with the archival images, I created a series of collages of teeth and things that look like teeth (gemstones, mushrooms, root vegetables), presented in a flower-fold book – it opens like a mouth – and a concertina-collage of teeth and mouths. These two experiments were never intended to be reproduced within the final print-on-demand edition; they were processes of *thinking through making* as I was considering how to illustrate the essays. You can see how my juxtaposed images of teeth and things that look like teeth in the flower-fold book led to the final illustrations of a tooth/lemon and tooth/crab.

Finally, the last anti-chapter was a book called *Analogue Emails*. It starts with a short essay I wrote describing the long history of published collections of letters that document writer-artist collaborations (such as *I Send You This Cadmium Red*, correspondence between John Christie and John Berger), and expressing my concern that in a digital age, this kind of documentation of creative collaborations may disappear. I transcribed every email Tom and I sent to each other, including the meta-data listing email title, time sent, and attachments. This unedited, personal correspondence allows Tom and I to reflect on our collaboration, and invites others to observe the usually private process of taking a project from an initial idea (when Tom sent me a draft of the 'foot' essay and I responded 'of course I want to make a foot book' to the last email, sent 16 months later, telling Tom I had to send the file to print).

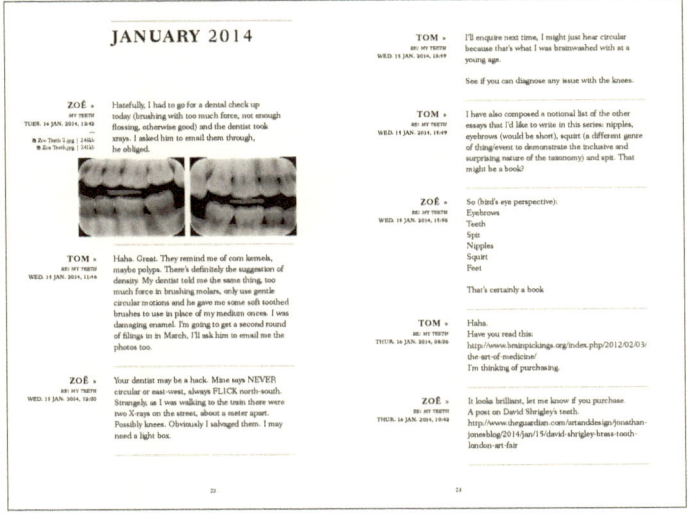

Spread from
Analogue Emails

PRODUCTION DETAILS

From the beginning of the project I intended to produce a print-on-demand edition of these books. Earlier collaborations between Tom and I were sought after by friends and colleagues, and I suspected this one would be popular. I didn't have time to finish the design and test print before the Writers' Festival, so I handmade the first set. However, planning ahead, I chose formats (size and shape) based on **BLURB** template sizes: the larger book is a 'standard portrait' (200 x 250mm) and the smaller books are 'pocket' (130 x 120mm). The flower-fold and concertina books were intended to be limited-edition artists' books, not for commercial reprinting.

The opposite page shows a material and cost break down for the handmade versus print-on-demand editions of the main book (the standard portrait).

The handmade one is undoubtedly more desirable from an aesthetic perspective. The uncoated cover stock and red tape (from the thermal binding) are more tactile and subtle than the high gloss print-on-demand cover – which was the only paper back option available in this format. However, the cost of producing a single edition demonstrates the financial imperative for print-on-demand over handmade editions.

Analogue Bodies Vol. 1

HANDMADE EDITION
BY ME

—

FORMAT
Thermal bound paperback, 48pp
210 x 260mm (standard portrait)

STOCK
Pages: 148gsm Mohawk Options
Cover: 200gsm Canson, black
Cream endpapers

PRODUCTION COST
Printing: $45.00
Paper stock: $25.90
Sub-total: **$70.90**

POSTAGE + HANDLING*
Local $7.20
Overseas $14.10

—

TOTAL: **$78.10 / $85.00**

* Note that 'handling' – my time
corresponding with a customer, taking
the book to the post office, etc. – is not
factored into this, nor is my production
time –printing, cropping and binding
the book.

Analogue Bodies Vol. 1

PRINT-ON-DEMAND EDITION (Paperback)
BLURB BOOKS

—

FORMAT
Perfect bound paperback, 48pp
210 x 260mm (standard portrait)

STOCK
Pages: 148gsm 'Premium Matte'
Cover: Standard gloss
 No endpaper option

PRODUCTION COST
Unit price: $19.70
+ tax $3.37
Sub-total: **$23.07**

POSTAGE + HANDLING
To Australia $13.99

—

TOTAL: **$37.06**

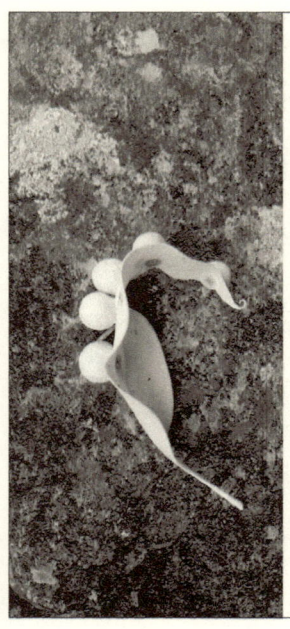

Over three days in late January 2013,
poet Tom Lee walked illustrator Zoë
Sadokierski and photographer Jacquie
Lorber-Kasunic around Coorah, his
family farm in central west NSW.

WORDS FROM THE FIRST WALK
tells the story of the walk in three ways:
the poet retraces past memories; the
illustrator obsesses with the minutiae of
shape, colour and pattern; the photographer maps movement in the landscape
brought about by farming practices.

FRONT COVER: BACK COVER:
BIRD BOOK 3   LEAF BOOK
Zoë Sadokierski Zoë Sadokierski
2013   2013

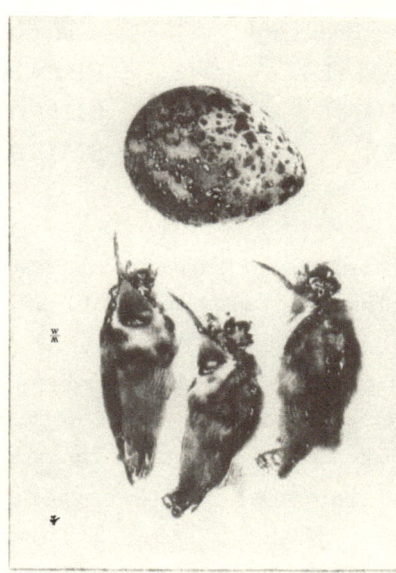

A POET WALKS
AN ILLUSTRATOR &
A PHOTOGRAPHER
AROUND A FARM

WORDS
FROM
THE
FIRST
WALK

2013

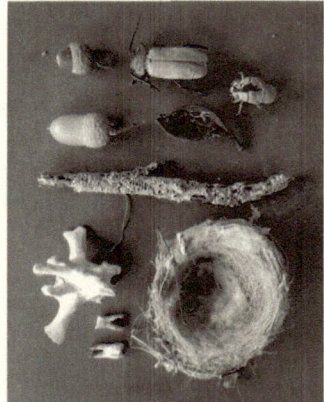

2009 / 2013

WORDS AND IMAGES

ZOË SADOKIERSKI

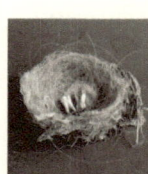

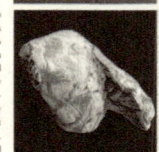

I first visited Coorah in 2009, on a writing retreat. I arrived with
no expectations of the place, other than the opportunity to work
on my thesis with as few distractions as possible. Months
earlier Astrid, Tom and I spent three productive days writing in a
house on the coast. Although I was a year further into my doctoral
research than the others, I am a less experienced writer. I vaguely
believed my productivity on the coast was due to a skill-transfer-
by-osmosis that occurred by being near Tom and Astrid as they
wrote. I wanted to replicate the magic. Arriving at Coorah that first
time, I was DEEPLY SELF ABSORBED, affected by 'thesis madness'.
The land, and life the Lee family bring to it, were an unexpected
delight. Vivid images stay with me from the trip:

> Astrid and I shared a room in the cottage. We laughed
> like city kids on school camp because a couple of
> stray sheep were making weirdly human noises
> outside our window. Tom called out periodically from
> the next room, to find out what all the fuss was about.

11

WORDS
FROM THE
FIRST WALK

—

Essays and visual essays by
Tom Lee, Zoë Sadokierski
& Jacquie Lorber-Kasunic

PROJECT DESCRIPTION

This book documents the project *Words from the First Walk.*
Over three days in late January 2013, poet Tom Lee walked
illustrator Zoë Sadokierski and photographer Jacquie Lorber
Kasunic around his family farm, Coorah in central west New

South Wales. Tom described the land and named the places
and things on it while Jacquie and Zoë documented, in their
own ways. The party moved from landmark to landmark:
bumping about in the ute, pushing through burr-starred
paddocks, scrabbling up rocks scabbed with lichen, entering
into and emerging from atmospheres of light, sound, surface
and weather; always accompanied by the various non-hu-
mans that also lay claim to the land, always wondering at the
different ways the land had been greeted and praised in the
long history of its habitation.

    The book tells the story of a walk, in three ways. The poet
retraces past memories; two of Tom's essays about Coorah are
presented within. The photographer maps movement in the
landscape brought about by farming practices; Jacquie created
a photo-essay from the walk. The illustrator obsesses with the
minutiae of shape and pattern; Zoë produced a collection of
collages, solar plate etchings and drawings that respond to a
passage from Murray Bail's novel *Eucalyptus.*

The work was originally presented as an exhibition at the NG Art Popup gallery in Chippendale, 11–27 July 2013. Zoë also designed an exhibition catalogue, which was later developed into a stand-alone book. The book version was shortlisted for an Australian Book Design Award in 2014, in the 'Indie 1000' category.

PROJECT AIMS

Collectively, our research aims were to:

present alternate narratives of the same site, telling the story of a place through different media (poetry, essay writing, photography, print-making, book-making) and different authorial voices.

My aim in designing the catalogue was **to document the work shown in the 2013 exhibition, and provide context for the project and our individual practices through written statements** from all three collaborators about each of our motivations and processes.

My aim in designing the book after the exhibition was to *explain how the project extends beyond the exhibited work*. I wrote additional critical analysis of the research methods used, and included more process images to show how the work developed in process.

DESIGN STRATEGY

Simple typography and clean layout to encourage reading the longer essays, and minimal graphic elements around images to foreground the creative work. Each contributor was assigned a colour (Tom blue; Jacquie aqua; Zoë red) used on the work titles, page numbers, and pull quotes to visually distinguish between narrative voices in the different sections.

I illustrated Tom's essay with photographs I snapped of the things he was describing as we walked. These images are positioned down the margins of his essay, occasionally taking up a full page if particularly relevant to the written description. I also included sketches from my diary and notes I took to remind myself of the walk later, which I though may add extra information to help readers understand things like mistletoe birds and types of trees. These images are treated differently than Jacquie's photographic essay, which I laid out very simply, with no unnecessary type or image on the pages to detract from the narratives within the photographs themselves.

PRODUCTION DETAILS

PRINT-ON-DEMAND SUPPLIER: **Lulu.com**
FORMAT:
189 x 245.8 mm (Crown Quatro), 90 pp.
Gloss cover, matt internal pages

Ordering additional books from the same files previously supplied I found significant differences in the colour reproduction on the cover, and in addition, the same 'standard matte' paper stock is notably different from one edition to the next. *Inconsistency such as these are a problem with print-on-demand services – particularly for reproducing art or photographic work where colour and paper-texture can change the look and feel of the content.*

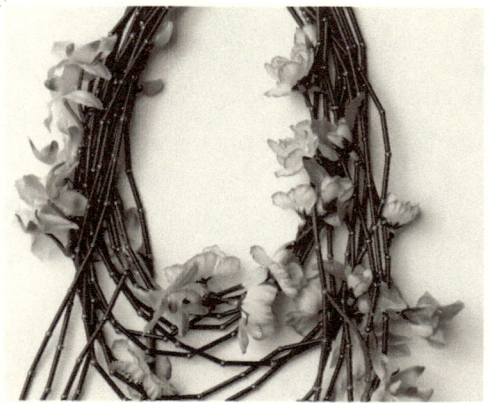

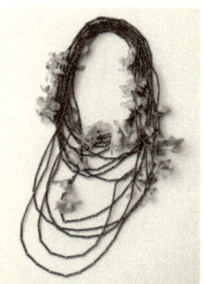

NECKLACE: Wine of the Gods
MATERIAL: Silk, Floral Objects, Beads, Oxidised Brass
DIMENSION: 1000mm
PHOTO: Mariano and Ellen, I Love Street
YEAR: 2013

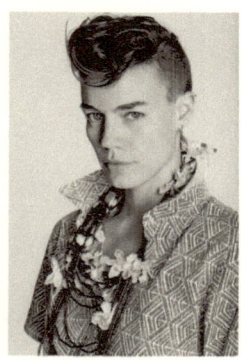

TITLE: Elliot
PHOTO: Mariano and Ellen, I Love Street
YEAR: 2014

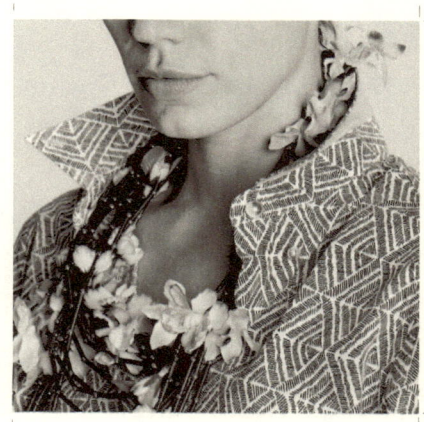

ZOË SADOKIERSKI
BOOK DESIGNER AND ILLUSTRATOR

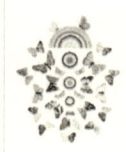

Zoë and I have a long standing friendship and share years of collaboration, including her illustrating quirky bird stickers for a leather-themed jewelry collection and realizing a tattoo for me, in exchange for a bracelet. We work tremendously together; her outlook on the world speaks to my humor. Her innate understanding of my aesthetic were key ingredients to our collaboration for the catalogue for Mariposa. Working on the catalogue concurrent with developing the pieces opened for me a new dialogue about the collaborative process.

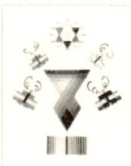

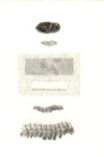

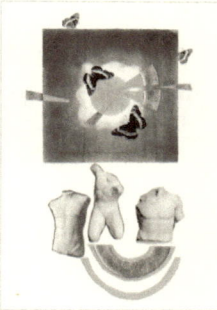

TITLES:
Mariposa 1. Butterflies Rest
Mariposa 2. Attract and Sustain
Mariposa 3. Relaunch
Mariposa 4. Sex and Death
MATERIALS: Digital Image Line Icon
www.whitepaperarchitects.com cut paper
DESCRIPTION: Prayer cataloges
YEAR: 2014

MARIPOSA

*Catalogue for a collection
of jewelry by* George Plionis

—

Written text by George Plionis;
photography by I Love Shoot,
design & illustrations by
Zoë Sadokierski

DESCRIPTION

This book is the catalogue for *Mariposa*, a collection of jewelry by George Plionis presented at Fitzgerald Jewelry, Brooklyn (NY), June 20 – Aug 29 2014. Mariposa means both butterfly and homosexual in a specific cultural context; George explains that the collection:

> *invites us to 'try gender on' and as a result,*
> *just be with the work, regardless of who we are*
> *and how we ordinarily perceive ourselves.*

It includes collaborations with: ceramic artist Andrew Robinson; fashion designer Timo Rissanen; photographer Mariano Garcia and stylist Ellen Schiavone Pande-Rolfsen (I Love Shoot) and; illustrator and book designer Zoë Sadokierski.

PROJECT AIMS

George wanted a catalogue for his jewelry exhibition that showcased each piece, and documented the creative collaborations he initiated as part of his design process. In the introduction George explains that through collaboration, he explores:

Interdisciplinary relationships with seemingly dispa-rate practitioners to discover how cross-pollination of craft and design principles can affect the design process and see what forms the outcome might make.

For me, the project provided an opportunity to **test how I could design and produce a catalogue in Sydney for an exhibition happening in New York on a tight deadline, using print-on-de-mand services.** My earlier print-on-demand experiments had no real deadline, and this project had a dangerously tight turn around. I received the initial batch of images May 27, the written text June 6, final images June 8 and sent the book to print June 10. In this 18-day period I was also juggling teaching and two other research projects. The tight schedule made print-on-demand an appealing option because I was unable to quickly source a reliable printer in NY, and printing with a Sydney company then posting the books would involve negotiation and running around time I did not have.

This project also provided an opportunity to continue exploring how I can use images with creative commons licenses as part of my illustration practice. See also: *Analogue Bodies*; the Seizure novella covers.

DESIGN STRATEGY

Three primary communication aims drove my design process:

1. To *foreground the photographs of George's jewelery by using clean, simple typography and few graphic elements* on the pages showcasing the final work. Respecting the work of the photographer and stylist, I didn't want to interfere with their images other than cropping to show detail or juxtaposing for visual impact.

2. To *visually emphasise the key stories behind the collection*, which George explained via email were: *butterflies coming to rest*; *food for thought*; and *eggs in abundance*. To do so, I created collages to illustrate each of these themes, which I used to organise the catalogue into sections according to theme. These collages were crafted using scraps of cut-paper and printouts of butterfly and other images that I sourced from online archives of images in the public domain (free to reuse, even commercially) because the copyright has expired. Using these existing images sped up my image making process significantly; I collage more quickly than I draw if the subject is unfamiliar to me, or inaccessible to study from life.

3. To *explain how the collaborations informed George's creative process,* through a series of double-page spreads with short descriptions George wrote about each of the collaborators and process images. I used a busier layout with more images per spread to distinguish between the documentation of George's final work and this messier process .

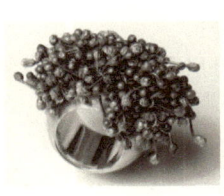

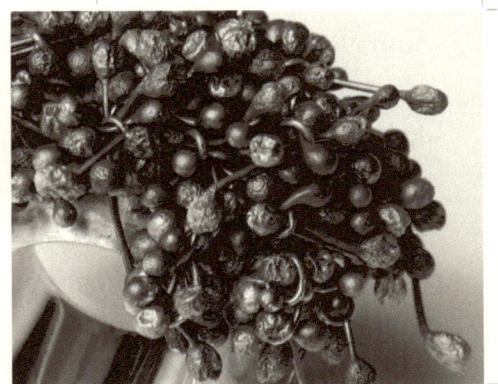

spread showing final work

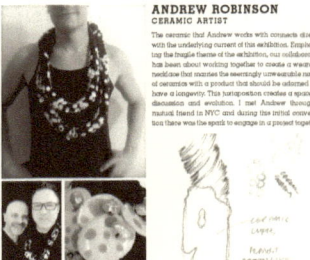

ANDREW ROBINSON
CERAMIC ARTIST

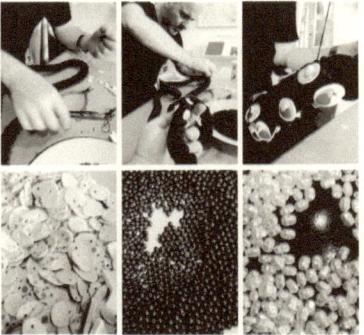

spread showing collaboration

PRODUCTION DETAILS

The catalogue was produced in a short run of 40 to sell at the gallery, with the intention of later creating a more substantial book, including critical reviews of the work and documentation of the work in situ, at a later date. The catalogue was also available to purchase online, for those unable to visit the exhibition in person, particularly relevant for an established Australian practitioner showing work in NY.

Lulu.com was chosen over Blurb.com as a print-on-demand service provider based on production times: Lulu promised a 3-5 working day turnaround, Blurb a 15 working day turnaround. Lulu delivered the books in 4 working days. *For exhibition catalogues, where images of final artwork often arrive at the last minute, a few days leeway in delivery can mean the difference between having books on opening night or not – the catalogue is most valuable at the busiest time.*

PRINT-ON-DEMAND SUPPLIER: Lulu.com
FORMAT: Perfect bound 19.05cm square. 50pp.
COVER: Full-colour ink on 100# weight white (gloss) paper.
INTERNAL: Full-colour ink on 80# weight white paper.

Turn around 3-5 business days.

On this book, there was a green tint to the photographs. The same thing happened on the *Words from the First Walk* book. Scanning online forums, I found this is a common problem, but I didn't want to colour correct the images – especially a professional photographers studio portraits – in case the problem was fixed. Colour matching is crucial for exhibition catalogues, but so is getting a book printed on time and on a tight budget. **Concessions have to be made, and print quality seems to be one of them.**

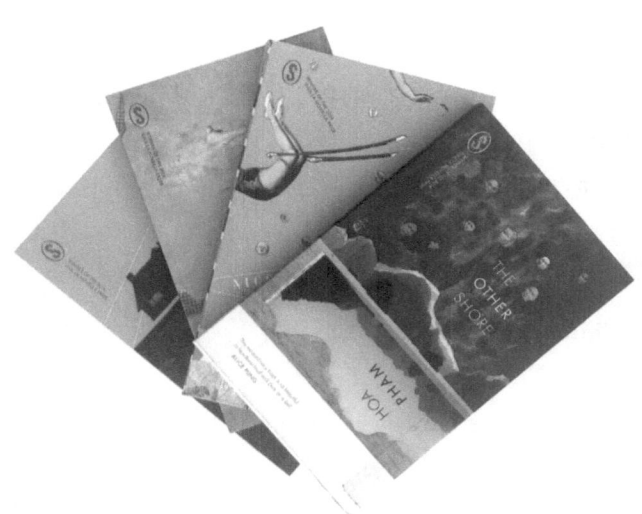

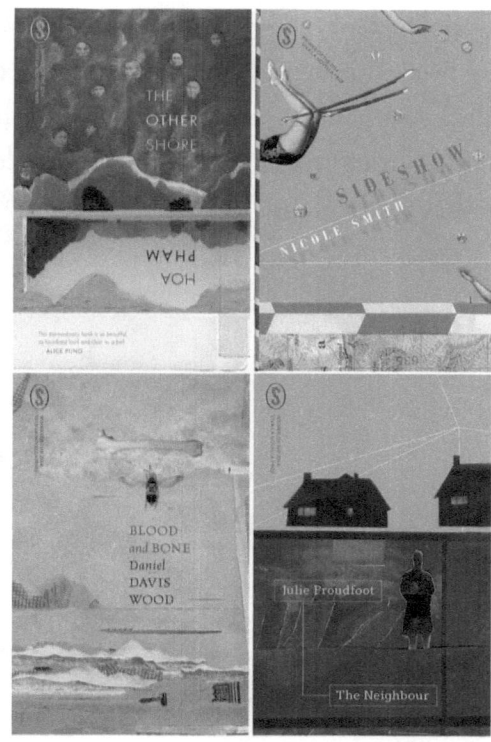

VIVA LA NOVELLA SERIES

—

Four book cover designs for independent Australian publisher Seizure, 2014

DESCRIPTION

Seizure is creative collective and an independent Australian publisher. Now in its second year, Seizure's 'Viva La Novella' competition allows four emerging editors to each chose a novella from the 150 competitions entries, and work with their chosen author through 'an intensive development and editorial process'. The project is sponsored by the Copyright Agency Cultural Fund.

I designed the four covers for the 2014 competition without payment, on the condition that there would be minimal creative input about the design from anyone involved, so that I could extend my research into designing with Creative Commons licensed material.

These books may seem out of place in the context of the Books On Demand exhibition, however they were producing using print-on-demand service Lightening Source. Many small publishers use print-on-demand in order to print a small run of books to test whether there is a market for the relatively unknown author/s. If the book sells well, additional stock can quickly be ordered.

PROJECT AIM

Initially, my primary aim was to test how I could incorporate Creative Commons licensed images in a commercial design job. In particular, I was **testing** *how CC licensed images available through less reliable sources than museum and library archives – such as Flickr or Wikicommons images – could be incorporated in commercial design work.* See the aims attached to the *Analogue Bodies* project for more on my CC license research.

I designed the covers at around the same time I was working on the *Analogue Bodies* project, and realised in retrospect that this project afforded an opportunity to test how print-on-demand works within a commercial publishing project. Unlike the other book experiments in this collection in which I authored, designed and self-published the books, for this project I took the traditional role of designer within a network. The publisher (Seizure) chose the production house (Lightning Source) and specified the book size (trade paperback) and production specifications (full-colour cover with a satin/matte-lamination).

43.

—

DESIGN STRATEGY

This is an unusual design project. A set of books is usually published as a 'series' because they are connected by place, theme or author – the designer uses the connection between the books to inform the design of the series. These four books are only connected because they were each selected by one of the editors in the competition. As a way to make a connection between the four unconnected books, I decided to impose a material constraint on myself – I only used cut-paper collage to illustrate the covers. I printed images that were available under Creative Commons licenses – such as the acrobat's legs on the *Sideshow* cover – and collaged them with collected ephemera and paper textures. This connection will probably go unnoticed by most viewers, but the strategy of designing all four covers using the same collage technique was important to my creative process, providing a link that helped me design each cover so it communicates the unique content of each book, while holding together as a series. This process warrants further description, but elsewhere.

PRODUCTION DETAILS

The limitations of print-on-demand had little effect on my
design process. As with most commercial fiction design
briefs, I was not able to chose the format (trade publishing
has set sizes for different types of books, a designer rarely
choses the format) and the printing constraints are the same
as any book with a tight budget (full-colour printing, no extra
embellishments such as foil, embossing or spot colours). In
a commercial context, it made no difference to me as a
designer whether the publisher used a traditional book
printer or a print-on-demand service for a fiction book with a
tight budget.

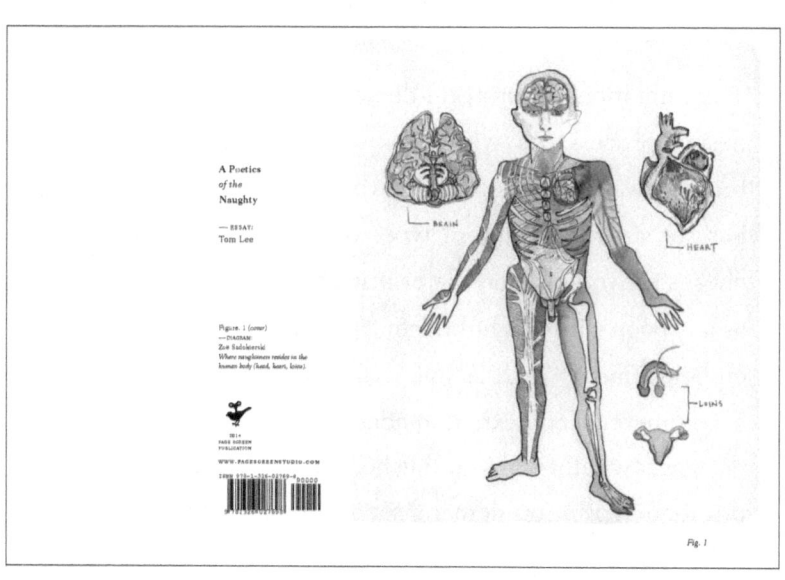

A Poetics
of the
Naughty

— ESSAY:
Tom Lee

BRAIN

HEART

Figure. 1 (cover)
—DIAGRAM:
Zoë Sadokierski
Where naughtiness resides in the
human body (hand, heart, loins).

LOINS

2011
PAGE SCREEN
PUBLICATION

WWW.PAGESCREENSTUDIO.COM

ISBN 978-1-326-03720-8

Fig. 1

THE EFFORT TO ADD,

CONCEPTUALLY
AND # POETICALLY,

TO THE RANGE   OF WAYS WE
IDENTIFY   ACTIVITY,
AND TO ENSURE THAT OUR   MEANS OF IDENTIFICATION
ARE SUITABLY

INFORMATIVE,   USEFUL AND
INTERESTING.

A POETICS OF THE NAUGHTY.

Essay by Tom Lee

—

meddled with by
Zoë Sadokierski

DESCRIPTION

'A Poetics of the Naughty' is an essay written by Tom Lee, typeset and illustrated by Zoë Sadokierski. Tom and Zoë have been collaborating for several years to make illustrated books on ridiculous topics (see also: the *Analogue Bodies* project, forthcoming 'Poetics of the Creepy'). Tom's essay covers biblical naughty figs, trickster god Hermes, what naughty animals and children get up to, and Kafka's mischievous characters.

PROJECT AIMS

Within the essay, Tom states his mission is to:

> *add, conceptually and poetically, to the range of ways we identify activity, and to ensure that our means of identification are suitably informative, useful and interesting.*

My aim was to get Tom's delightful essay into the hands of more readers, considering:

how could I materialise the essay as a
visually appealing publication,
without overdesigning it to the point
that it becomes a thing to look at
rather than to read.

DESIGN STRATEGY

In order to encourage deep reading, most of the typesetting is classic and unobtrusive (it looks like books you've seen before – familiarity puts a reader at ease), with generous white space on the page to prevent the text looking overly dense or difficult. There are two exceptions to the understated typesetting. First, a few pull quotes (significantly enlarged phrases) intend to grab the reader's attention at a flick through. Second, in the final section on Kafka's characters from *The Castle*, huge glyphs (a hieroglyphic character or symbol) obscure parts of the written text. I couldn't design an essay on naughtiness without being a bit naughty; as Tom says: "It is a risky thing, to advocate naughtiness." The two Ø are visual metaphors for Kafka's characters Artur and Jeremias, misbehaving over the text as they do in Kafka's novel.

In the first iteration of this book (the zine version), one

reader suggested the final obscured page was too difficult to read. I knocked back the opacity of the black ink in the second edition; I'd rather be playfully naughty than annoying.

Another design consideration to make the essay more readable was typesetting footnotes small, running vertical to the main text to avoid disrupting the narrative on an initial read through. I think footnotes are for subsequent readings of a text like this; breadcrumbs, if you're still hungry.

The illustration depicting where naughtiness resides in the human body (an inside cover for the zine, the cover of the POD book) was my response to Tom's essay. I often illustrate a new idea in response to a text, using illustration as a way to visually extend the ideas within the text with new information. This creates a kind of dialogue between Tom's writing and my visualisation, very much like our collaboration in person.

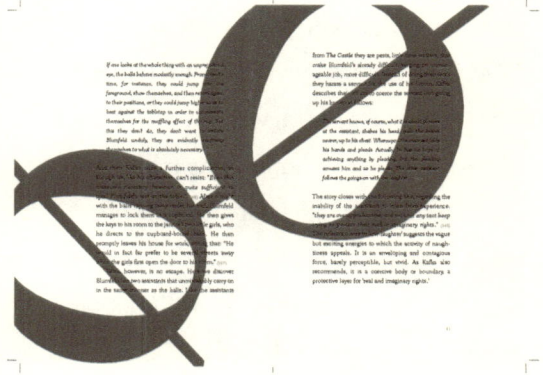

PRODUCTION DETAILS

This book is more expensive to produce print-on-demand, considering the first edition was laser printed on cheap stock. Bulk ordering would reduce the unit price by lowering the postage cost per book, but this leaves me *having to manage distribution myself, which defeats the purpose of using print-on-demand as a publishing model.*

A *Poetics of the Naughty* **HANDMADE** *BY ME*	A *Poetics of the Naughty* **PRINT-ON-DEMAND** *LULU BOOKS*
FORMAT	FORMAT
Saddle stitched (stapled), 48pp	Perfect bound paperback, 48pp
148 x 210mm (A5)	148 x 210mm (A5)
STOCK	STOCK
Pages: black laser on copy paper	Pages: black in k on 60# white'
Cover: 200gsm fluorescent orange	Cover: Full-colour on 100# (gloss)
Black laser inside cover.	No endpaper option
Hand numbered in pen on front	
PRODUCTION COST	PRODUCTION COST
Paper/print: $3.00	*Print/production* $4.54
POSTAGE + HANDLING*	POSTAGE + HANDLING
Prepaid envelop $1.70	Mail $7.99
TOTAL: **$4.70**	TOTAL: **$12.53**

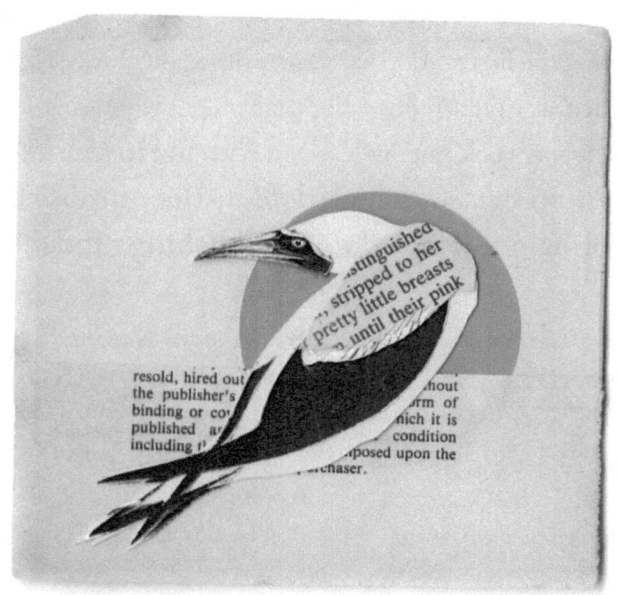

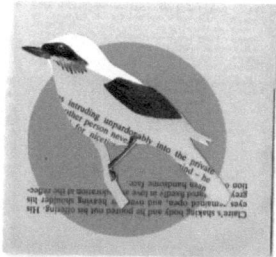

10   Moustached Flowerpiercer
Diglossa mystacalis

BIRDS *WITH* SMUTTY NAMES

—

Illustrations by
Zoë Sadokierski

DESCRIPTION

Birds With Smutty Names depicts 20 birds with names that prove ornithologists have a sense of humour, from the Agile Tit-Tyrant to the Moustached Flowerpiercer. Each bird is illustrated using collaged pages from an erotic novel.

The original 'smutty birds' idea came from a conversation with Timo Rissanen in 2009, and I created the illustrations in 2012 as part of the Unlikely Avian Taxonomies project, a collaboration with my colleague Kate Sweetapple. The illustrations were presented on an A2 poster, as part of a series of actual birds re-categorised based on patterns in their names.

PROJECT AIM

To produce a high-quality book version of my smutty bird illustrations, considering: how could I encourage the viewer to see each bird individually and observe the detail in the collage materials.

DESIGN STRATEGY

The collages were created using photographs of each bird (sourced online, printed black-and-white on copy paper), orange tracing paper, and pages from Anne-Marie Villefranche's novel *Folies D'Amour: An erotic memoir of Paris in the 1920s*, which I acquired in a second-hand bookstore for $2.

The text from the novel that appears on the body of each bird directly relates to its smutty name. For instance, the Agile Tit-Tyrant contains the word 'breast'.

It's difficult to read the detail in each collage in relation to the bird name in the A2 poster version of the work. This book version allows each collage to be viewed in isolation, giving the viewer more space to consider the relationship between words (bird name) and the illustration.

PRODUCTION DETAILS:

PRINT-ON-DEMAND SUPPLIER: **Blurb.com**

FORMAT: Hardcover dust-jacket, standard black linen. Proline charcoal endsheets. Proline uncoated paper. 180mm square. 44pp.

COST: $49.94 + 4.99 tax
        $13.50 shipping
        $68.43

Ordered 23 Sept; shipped 28 Sept; arrived 7 Oct

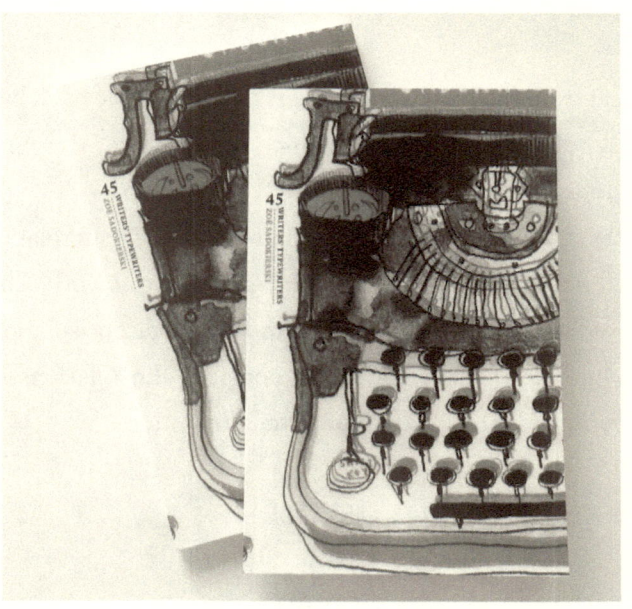

LEONARD COHEN
Olivetti Lettera 32
1934 —
· · · · · · · · ·

In 1964, Cohen rented a small room in a
house on Pine Street in Montreal. He poured
pine oil into his bath, staining the water the
same colour as his Olivetti. Inspired, he took
his typewriter into the bath and tried to type
underwater. Dissatisfied with the result he
threw it against the wall. When the store clerk
laughed at him cradling his broken typewriter,
Cohen wandered out to the work room and
asked an old man tinkering with machines to
help. A few days later he returned to find the
typewriter restored.

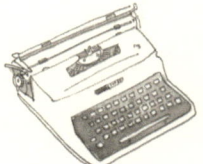

WRITERS
TYPEWRITERS

—

Illustrations by
Zoë Sadokierski

DESCRIPTION

Writers' Typewriters presents anecdotes about 45 famous writers' creative process, alongside drawings of their actual typewriters. I drew from photographs of the typewriters sourced from auction catalogues, library and museum archives and fan pages of the authors working with or posing next to their machines. I compiled the anecdotes from interviews, biographies and published letters.

For example, Leonard Cohen had a bath with his; it ended predictably poorly. Cormac McCarthy bought a second-hand Olivetti for $50 and sold it 46-years later for $254,500. Larry McMurtry thanked his Hermes 3000 in his Golden Globe acceptance speech for the *Brokeback Mountain* screenplay. A Catholic priest told Anne Sexton, "God is in your typewriter." Raymond Chandler declared: "Throw up into your typewriter every morning. Clean up every noon."

The original drawings, and an offset lithographic print of the drawings, were shown in Type Horses – an exhibition held at Blank_Space gallery (Surry Hills) in August 2011.

PROJECT AIM

To illuminate the relationship writers have with their writing machines, as part of an **ongoing consideration into the way tools affect creative practice**.

DESIGN STRATEGY

Typewriters are idiosyncratic objects – each brand and model is unique. As I studied each machine, and thought about the character of the author who owned it, I started attributing personalities to the machines themselves. I decided to illustrate the typewriters alone, without context (the desk or other location) or subjects (the authors themselves), to draw attention to the individual character of each machine. Paired with information naming the writer, the model, the writer's lifespan and a short passage about the writer's relationship with the machine, the typewriters are celebrated as collaborators in the creative process. I challenge you to look at Kafka's machine without thinking of Metamorphosis.

PRODUCTION DETAILS

PRINT-ON-DEMAND SUPPLIER: Blurb.com
FORMAT: Perfect-bound paperback, pocket (130 x 200cm), economy cream trade B&W paper, matte finish. 94pp.